THE JOURNAL

OF

AWESOME

by Neil Pasricha

CHRONICLE BOOKS
SAN FRANCISCO

Text and illustrations copyright © 2012 by Neil
Pasricha

ISBN 978-1-4521-0844-5

Manufactured in China

Illustrations by Monsieur Cabinet

10 9 8 7 6

Chronicle Books publishes distinctive books and
gifts. From award-winning children's titles,
best-selling cookbooks, and eclectic pop culture
to acclaimed works of art and design, stationery,
and journals, we craft publishing that's instantly
recognizable for its spirit and creativity. Enjoy our
publishing and become part of our community at
www.chroniclebooks.com.

Chronicle Books LLC
680 Second Street
San Francisco, CA 94107

Hi everyone,

A few years ago I hit some giant speed bumps in life. Within the span of a few months, my wife told me she didn't love me anymore and my best friend lost the battle with serious illness. I was heartbroken and lonely, and my mind was all over the place.

I found a lot of comfort back then in **writing** about one awesome thing every single day. I would come home from work and start jotting notes about random little things—like the cold side of the pillow, **the smell of a bakery**, or finding five bucks in my coat pocket—and just sort of smile to myself.

Over time these awesome things started putting my mind in a different place. They helped me get to bed without a twisted stomach. They helped me focus on all the little things that make life so awesome.

So I kept coming home and writing about one awesome thing every day. I kept writing and writing and writing until my little website called **1000 Awesome Things** suddenly won some big awards and got published as *The Book of Awesome* and then *The Book of (Even More) Awesome* and then *The Book of (Holiday) Awesome* in dozens of countries and languages around the world.

The *Journal of Awesome* was created in response to the teachers, preachers, grandparents, and grandkids who told me they started writing their own little thoughts about what made them **think, smile, and laugh** from their day.

This journal is a wide open space for you to share your big wishes, dream your big dreams, and remember all the **precious little moments** that make up your day. I've filled it up with **pictures**, **prompts**, and **reminders** of how awesome life can be. I know you've got lots of your own thoughts too, and I think that together we can create something pretty special.

LET'S HAVE SOME FUN AND LET'S STAY AWESOME FOREVER AND EVER AND EVER.

Love,
Neil

AWESOME!

What was the most
awesome part of
your day?

DATE _____

Breakfast for dinner

AWESOME!

When you hear
someone's smile
over the phone

Waking up and realizing it's your day off

AWESOME!

DATE _____

_____

_____

_____

_____

_____

_____

_____

_____

_____

_____

_____

_____

_____

_____

_____

_____

_____

_____

_____

Crossing something
off your to-do list

_____

_____

_____

_____

List three awesome
things you've never
noticed before.

_____

_____

_____

_____

_____

_____

_____

_____

_____

_____

_____

_____

_____

_____

When it feels like the
lyrics to the song
you're listening to were
written just for you

DATE _____

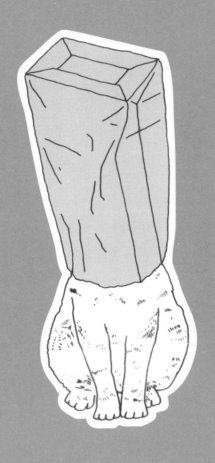

When cats do stupid
things

AWESOME!

_____

_____

_____

_____

_____

_____

_____

_____

_____

_____

_____

_____

_____

_____

Eating anything from

your own garden

Seeing a balloon
way up in the sky
somewhere

AWESOME!

Quick! What was the most awesome part of your week?

The moment on vacation when you forget what day of the week it is

Good mail days

AWESOME!

DATE _____

The grass is green,

the sky is blue,

the world is awesome,

and so are you

Finishing the workout

AWESOME!

What's one awesome thing
you want to do sometime
in your life?

The sound of ice cubes cracking in a drink

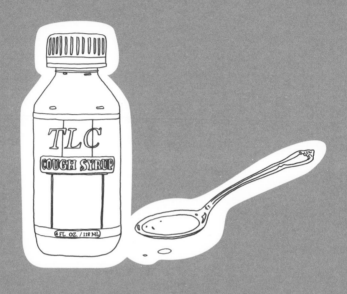

Having someone
take care of you when
you're sick

AWESOME!

_____

_____

_____

_____

_____

_____

_____

_____

_____

_____

_____

_____

_____

_____

_____

_____

_____

Turning off all
the lights during
a thunderstorm

Finding something
you lost years ago
wedged in the couch
cushions

AWESOME!

Who was the most
awesome person in
your life this week?
Bonus points if you
tell them!

Be you, be cool,
be awesome

Buddy's
Fictionary
A
to
Z

Making up new
words that only you
and your friends
understand

AWESOME!

DATE

_____

_____

_____

_____

_____

_____

_____

_____

_____

_____

_____

_____

_____

_____

_____

Celebrating your
pet's birthday even
though they have no
idea what's going on

When it's pouring
rain but you pass the
point of caring at all

AWESOME!

Pick someone you love being around! Now, what are three awesome traits you love about them?

Dangling your feet
in water

Snagging all the
free stuff from hotel
rooms

AWESOME!

DATE _____

When your pet notices
you're in a bad mood
and comes to see you

hello
sweetie

Grandma emails

AWESOME!

What are three awesome
traits you'd like to bring
out a bit more in yourself?

Laughing so hard you make no sound at all

Stretching your legs
after a really long
car ride

AWESOME!

_____

_____

_____

_____

_____

_____

_____

_____

_____

_____

_____

_____

_____

_____

_____

_____

_____

Psst. BEING ALIVE
IS PRETTY
AWESOME

Remembering to call your mom on her birthday

AWESOME!

List the awesome things
you noticed this week.
What was awesome
about them?

If you can make a
baby laugh today,
you are awesome

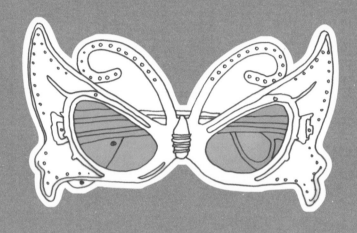

Trying on the most ridiculous sunglasses you can find at the store

AWESOME!

DATE _____

_____

_____

_____

_____

_____

_____

_____

_____

_____

_____

_____

_____

_____

_____

_____

_____

_____

_____

_____

When the hiccups stop

The first day of the
year you get to wear
shorts

AWESOME!

What is awesome
about your favorite
home-cooked meal?

The smell of rain on a hot sidewalk

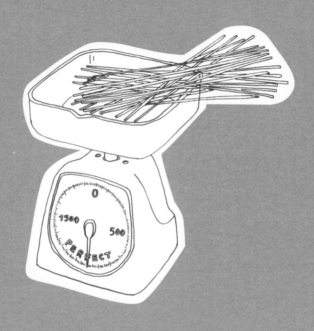

Actually making
the right amount of
spaghetti

AWESOME!

Pulling a weed
and getting all
the roots with it

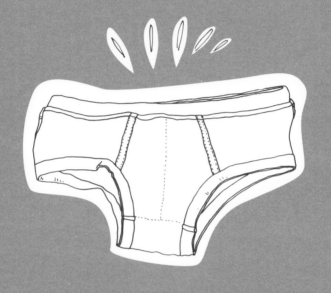

Your first day
in brand-new
underwear

AWESOME!

Go somewhere new today
and look for something
awesome.

Falling asleep in
the backseat of a
car late at night on
the drive home

Spotting your house
from the airplane
window

AWESOME!

Psst. TODAY IS
AWESOME!

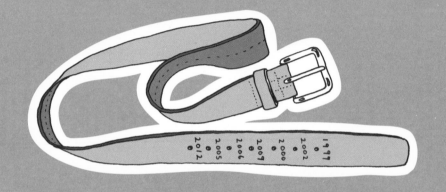

Moving down a notch
on your belt buckle

AWESOME!

When the vending machine gives you two things instead of one

Tell someone they are awesome today!

Hitting a string of
green lights in a row

Eating cookies way
past your bedtime

AWESOME!

Tripping and realizing
nobody saw you

Talking to little kids about what they want to be when they grow up

AWESOME!

DATE _____

Coming back to

your own bed

after a long trip

List awesome things you're grateful for today. How do they make you feel?

Finally peeing after holding it forever

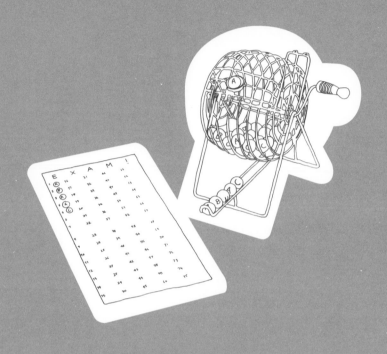

Completely guessing
the right answer on a
multiple choice test

AWESOME!

_____

_____

_____

_____

_____

_____

_____

_____

_____

_____

_____

_____

_____

_____

_____

_____

_____

_____

When you're close to
the end of a book

Watching home
movies

AWESOME!

If you could have lunch
with anyone in the world,
which awesome person
would you pick and why?

That one really weird food combination that only you love

DATE _____

When someone finds
your lost wallet and
returns it

AWESOME!

The smell of a bakery

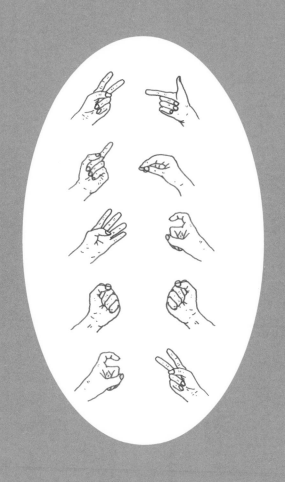

Secret handshakes

AWESOME!

When you manage
to squeeze out enough
toothpaste for one
last brush

DATE _____

Notice something
awesome today that
you've never noticed
before.

Fixing electronics
by smacking them

Jumping into a big pile of leaves

AWESOME!

The moment just
before you fall asleep
when you know you're
about to fall asleep

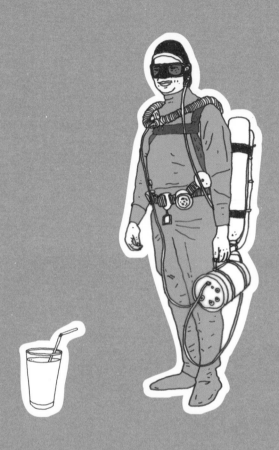

Blowing bubbles
in your milk

AWESOME!

DATE _____

Getting a card from
someone you thought
you'd lost touch with

Getting a glimpse
of the first parade
float coming around
the corner

AWESOME!

What was awesome about
your day?

AWESOME!